RUBANK EDUCATIONAL LIBRARY No. 95

FLUTE
Vol. I

H. VOXMAN
AND
WM. GOWER

AN OUTLINED COURSE OF STUDY
DESIGNED TO FOLLOW UP ANY
OF THE VARIOUS ELEMENTARY
AND INTERMEDIATE METHODS

HAL•LEONARD®
CORPORATION
7777 W. BLUEMOUND RD. P.O. BOX 13819 MILWAUKEE, WI 53213

NOTE

THE RUBANK ADVANCED METHOD for Flute is published in two volumes, the course of study being divided in the following manner:

Vol. I { Keys of C, F, G, B♭, and D Major.
{ Keys of A, D, E, G, and B Minor.

Vol. II { Keys of E♭, A, A♭, E, D♭, and B Major.
{ Keys of C, F♯, F, and C♯ Minor.

PREFACE

THIS METHOD is designed to follow any of the various Elementary and Intermediate instruction series, or Elementary instruction series comprising two or more volumes, depending upon the previous development of the student. The authors have found it necessary in their teaching experience to draw from many sources in order to provide a progressive course of study. The present publication assembles in two volumes, the material essential to a well-rounded musical development.

THE OUTLINES, one of which is included in each of the respective volumes, tend to afford an objective picture of the student's progress. They will facilitate the ranking of members in a large ensemble or they may serve as a basis for awards of merit. In addition, a one-sided development along strictly technical or strictly melodic lines is avoided. The use of these outlines, however, is not imperative and they may be discarded at the discretion of the teacher.

H. Voxman — Wm. Gower

OUTLINE
OF
RUBANK ADVANCED METHOD
FOR
FLUTE, Vol. I
BY
H. Voxman and Wm. Gower

UNIT	SCALES and ARPEGGIOS	(Key)	MELODIC INTERPRE-TATION	ARTICU-LATION	FINGER EXERCISES	ORNAMENTS	SOLOS	UNIT COM-PLETED
1	5 (1) 6 (5)	C	19 (1)	47 (1)	57 (1)	60 (1)	67 (1)	
2	5 (2) 6 (6)	C	20 (2)	47 (2)	57 (2)	60 (1)	67 (1)	
3	5 (3) 6 (7)	C	21 (3)	47 (3)	57 (3)	60 (2)	67 (1)	
4	6 (4) 6 (8)	C	22 (4)	48 (4)	57 (4)	60 (3)	67 (1)	
5	6 (9)	a	23 (5)	48 (5)	57 (5) (6)	60 (4)	67 (1)	
6	6 (10) 7 (12)	a	23 (5)	48 (6)	57 (7)	60 (5)	67 (1)	
7	7 (11) (13)	a	24 (6)	49 (7)	57 (8)	60 (6)	68 (2)	
8	7 (14) (15)	a	24 (6)	49 (8)	57 (9)	61 (7) (8)	68 (2)	
9	7 (16) 8 (20)	F	25 (7)	49 (9)	57 (10)	61 (9)	68 (2)	
10	8 (17) 9 (21)	F	25 (7)	49 (10)	57 (11)	61 (10) (11)	68 (2)	
11	8 (18) 9 (22)	F	27 (8)	50 (11)	57 (12)	61 (12)	68 (2)	
12	8 (19) 9 (23)	F	27 (8)	50 (12)	57 (13)	62 (13)	68 (2)	
13	9 (24)	d	28 (9)	50 (13)	57 (14)	62 (13)	69 (3)	
14	9 (25)	d	28 (10)	51 (14)	57 (15)	62 (14)	69 (3)	
15	9 (26) 10 (27) (28)	d	28 (10)	51 (14)	57 (16)	62 (15)	69 (3)	
16	10 (29) 11 (33)	G	30 (11)	51 (15)	57 (17) (18)	62 (16)	69 (3)	
17	10 (30) 11 (34)	G	31 (12)	51 (16)	57 (19)	62 (17)	69 (3)	
18	10 (31) 11 (35)	G	32 (13)	52 (17)	57 (20)	62 (18) 63 (19)	69 (3)	
19	11 (32) (36)	G	34 (14)	52 (18)	57 (21)	63 (20) (21)	70 (4)	
20	12 (37)	e	35 (15)	52 (19)	57 (22)	63 (22) (23)	70 (4)	
21	12 (38) (40)	e	36 (16)	53 (20)	57 (23) (24)	63 (24)	70 (4)	
22	12 (39) (41) (42)	e	36 (16)	53 (20)	57 (25)	63 (25)	70 (4)	
23	13 (43) 14 (47)	B♭	37 (17)	53 (21)	57 (26)	63 (26)	70 (4)	
24	13 (44) 14 (48)	B♭	37 (17)	53 (22)	57 (27)	63 (27)	70 (4)	
25	13 (45) 14 (49)	B♭	38 (18)	54 (23)	57 (28) (29)	64 (28)	71 (5)	
26	14 (46) (50)	B♭	38 (18)	54 (24)	57 (30)	64 (29) (30)	71 (5)	
27	14 (51)	g	39 (19)	54 (25)	57 (31)	65 (31)	71 (5)	
28	15 (52) (54)	g	40 (20)	54 (26)	57 (32)	65 (32)	71 (5)	
29	15 (53) (55) (56)	g	40 (20)	54 (26)	57 (33)	65 (33)	71 (5)	
30	16 (57) 17 (61)	D	41 (21)	55 (27)	57 (34)	65 (34)	71 (5)	
31	16 (58) 17 (62)	D	41 (21)	55 (28)	57 (35)	65 (35)	72 (6)	
32	16 (59) 17 (63)	D	42 (22)	56 (29)	57 (36)	65 (36)	72 (6)	
33	17 (60)	D	42 (22)	56 (29)	57 (37)	65 (37)	72 (6)	
34	17 (64)	b	43 (23)	56 (30)	57 (38)	66 (38)	72 (6)	
35	18 (65) (67)	b	44 (24)	56 (31)	57 (39)	66 (39)	72 (6)	
36	18 (66) (68) (69) (70)	b	44 (24)	56 (31)	57 (40)	66 (39)	72 (6)	

NUMERALS designate page number.
ENCIRCLED NUMERALS designate exercise number.
COMPLETED EXERCISES may be indicated by crossing out the rings, thus .

PRACTICE AND GRADE REPORT

FIRST SEMESTER

Student's Name _____ Date _____

Week	Sun.	Mon.	Tue.	Wed.	Thu.	Fri.	Sat.	Total	Parent's Signature	Grade
1	4/0	20	20	20	20	20	20	100		
2		25	15	20	20	20	20	100		
3		20	20	20	40	30		150		
4		20	20	20	20	10	20	130		
5		0	30							
6										
7										
8										
9										
10										
11										
12										
13										
14										
15										
16										
17										
18										
19										
20										

Semester Grade _____

Instructor's Signature _____

SECOND SEMESTER

Student's Name _____ Date _____

Week	Sun.	Mon.	Tue.	Wed.	Thu.	Fri.	Sat.	Total	Parent's Signature	Grade
1										
2										
3										
4										
5										
6										
7										
8										
9										
10										
11										
12										
13										
14										
15										
16										
17										
18										
19										
20										

Semester Grade _____

Instructor's Signature _____

Scales and Arpeggios
C Major

Copyright MCMXL by Rubank, Inc., Chicago, Ill.
International Copyright Secured

6

Various articulations may be used in the chromatic, the interval, and the arpeggio exercises at the option of the instructor.

Exercise in Thirds

Common Chord

Dominant 7th Chord

A Minor
The sign ∧ indicates a half step

Natural

Harmonic

Melodic

(1) Use $\frac{1}{T}$ $\frac{1}{E\flat}$ for A♯ (B♭) in all the chromatic scales.

(1) The student will find it advantageous to practice the flat scales using both the regular fingering and the B♭ key fingering for the B♭'s.

Common Chord
27
Diminished 7th
28
G Major
29
(1)
simile
30
simile
31
support air
more dynamics
This speed or little faster
hold out

(1) In very rapid passages F♯ may be fingered $\frac{1\ T\ 2\ 3}{2\ E\flat}$, but the practice should be discouraged.

E Minor

Dynamics
& support high notes

9/B

Bb Major

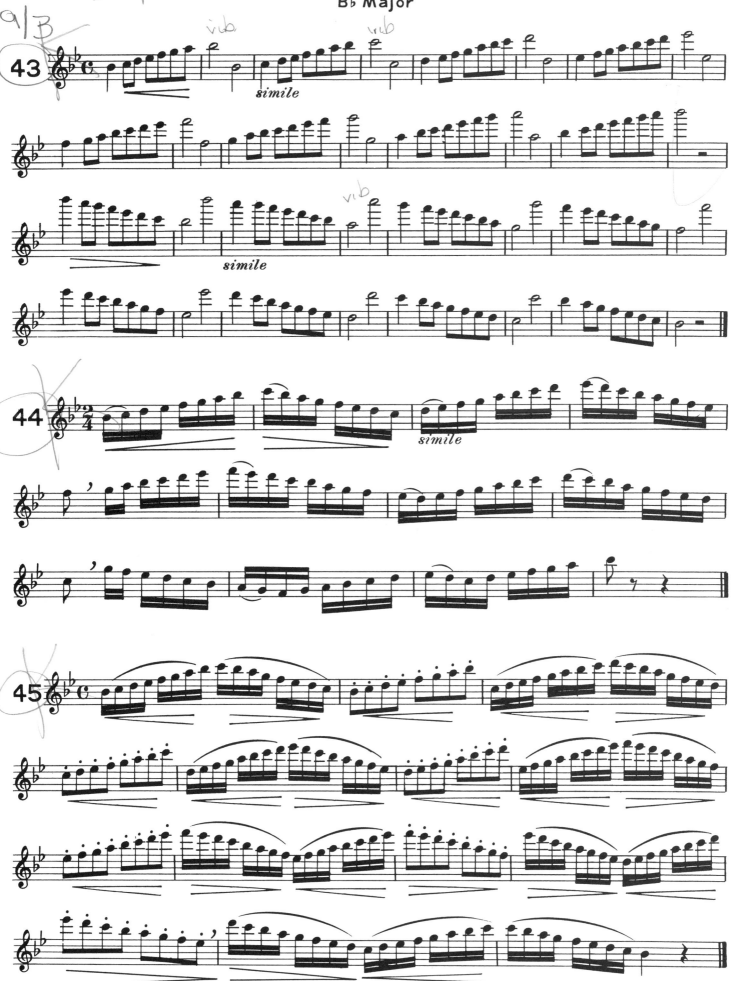

14

(1) High F# must be played with the single thumb key (T).

D Major

Studies in Melodic Interpretation

For One or Two Part Playing

The following studies are designed to aid in the development of the student's interpretative ability. Careful attention to the marks of expression is essential to effective use of the material. Pencil the technically difficult passages and devote extra time to their mastery.

In rhythmic music in the more rapid tempi (marches, dances, etc.) tones that are equal divisions of the beat are played somewhat detached (staccato). Tones that equal a beat or are multiples of a beat are held full value. Tones followed by rests are usually held full value. This point should be especially observed in slow music.

The *tenuto* sign (–) indicates the note is to be sustained full value.

HOHMANN

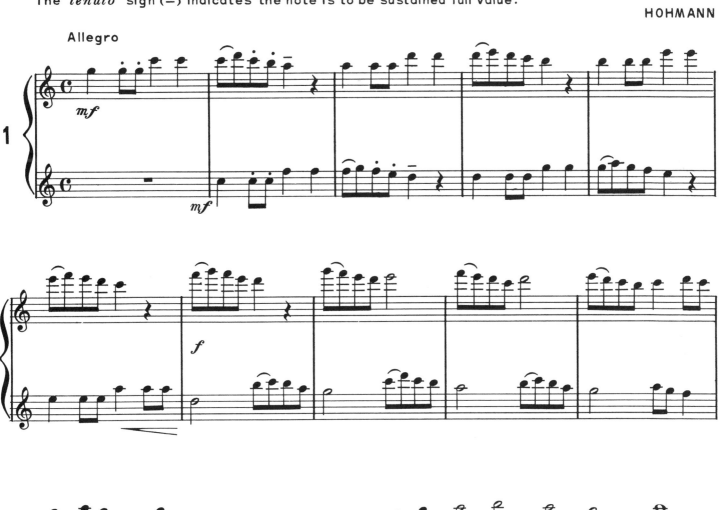

KUMMER

Allegretto

2

practice

Fine

lightly tone & separate

WIEDEMANN

Allegretto

Allegro

MOZART

Journey to the Moon (title)

Tempo di bolero (moderato)

TULOU

support your air

POPP

Allegro risoluto

Allegro

DEVIENNE

(1) See Ex. 7, page 61.

PLEYEL

Tempo di Menuetto

HOHMANN

Allegretto

KUMMER

Control sixteenth notes
metro.

Goal 100 = ♩

Allegretto

FODOR

14

CAMPAGNOLI

Allegro

16

Allegretto

17

Accents & Dynamics 3/25

18

Tempo di Polacca

SPOHR

DEVIENNE

Andantino

19

Adagio

SPOHR

HOHMANN

In No. 24 play the quarter and eighth notes somewhat detached. Give the syncopated notes a slight accent.

BÖHM

Allegro

24

Double Tonguing

The following two pages have not been made a regular part of the outline because it is not desirable to assign for all students the same time for beginning the study of these articulations. A correctly developed single tonguing is an essential prerequisite. If the student already possesses this ability, these studies may be begun at once. If he does not, they should be practiced only after further progress is made

Double tonguing is generally used only when single tonguing technic is inadequate. The articulation consists of a forward stroke of the tongue on T (tuh) and a backward one on K (kuh). Strive for a similar sharpness of attack on both consonants. Practice slowly until an even stroke of the tongue is acquired without a loss in tone quality.

Double tonguing is also applied to the rhythmic figure ♪♫ (or ♫♪) in rapid movements.

Triple Tonguing

This articulation consists of three motions of the tongue — on T, K, and T. The remarks concerning double tonguing apply here with equal force.

Studies in Articulation[1]

In all exercises where no tempo is indicated the student should play the study as rapidly as is consistent with tonal control and technical accuracy. The first practice on each exercise should be done very slowly in order that the articulation may be carefully observed.

In allegro tempi figures similar to should be performed , etc. The figure should be played .

The material for these exercises has been taken from the methods of Popp, Soussmann, Köhler, Gariboldi, etc.

These studies may be double tongued and single tongued after the preceding two pages have been mastered. Example , etc.

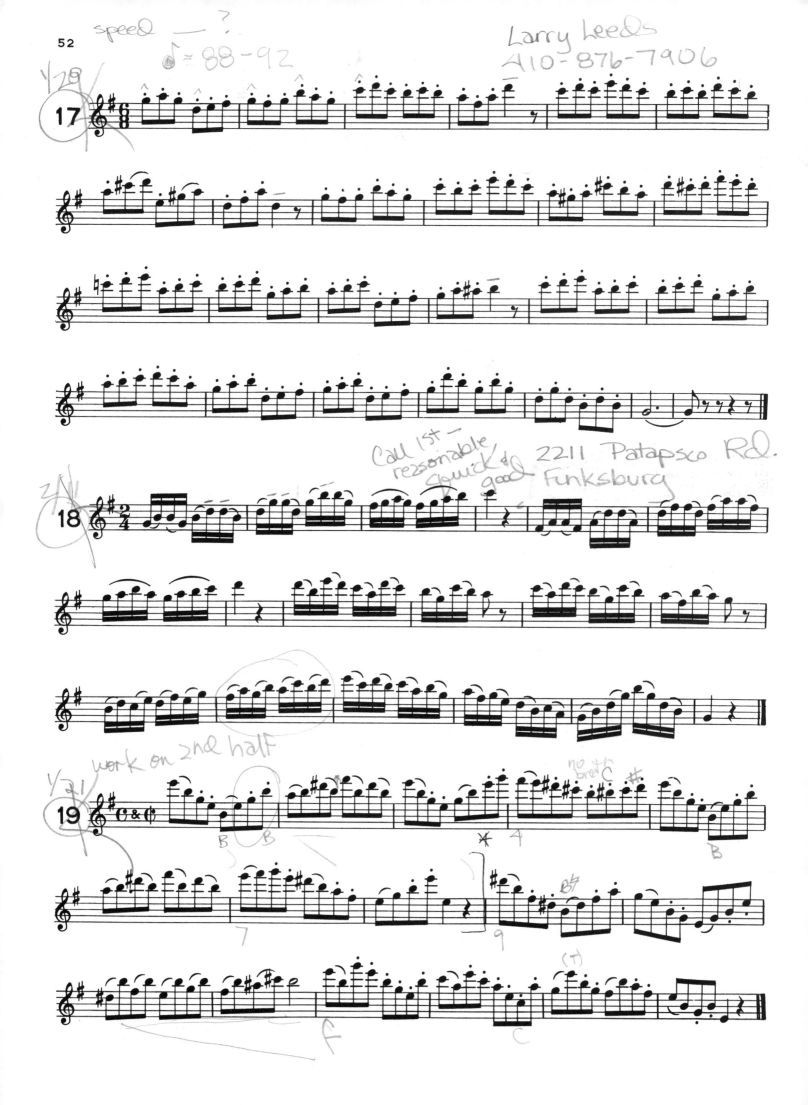

Exercises in Fingering

Practice these exercises slowly and increase in rapidity as the difficulties in fingering are over-come.

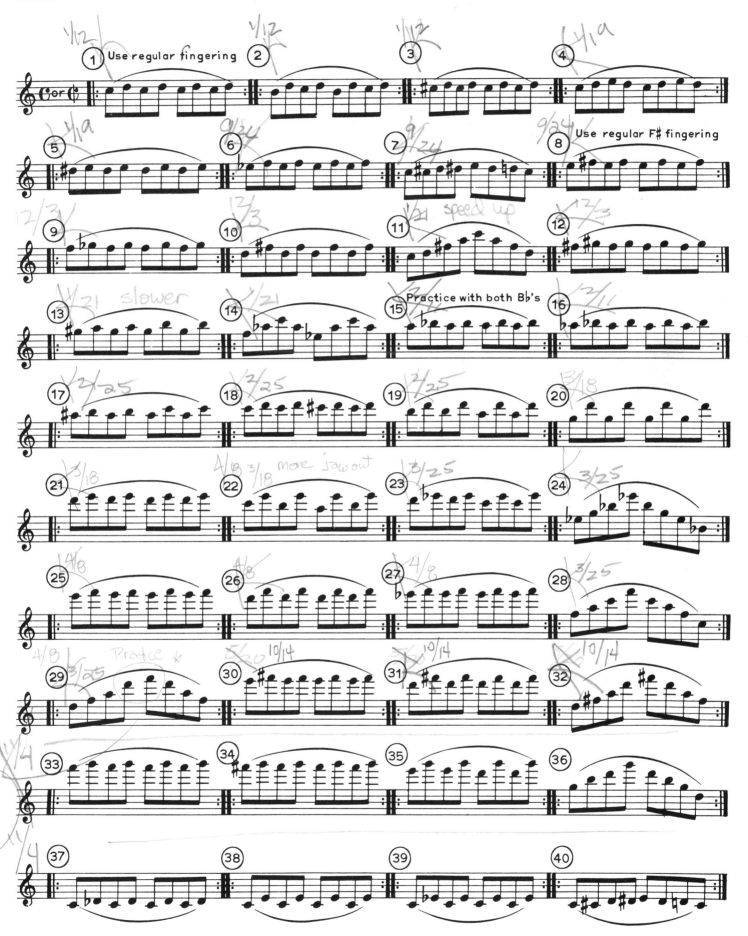

Table of Trills for the Boehm Flute (Closed G♯ Key)

Trill with finger pads or keys enclosed by ⩘ ⩘.

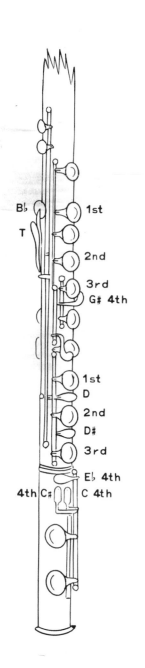

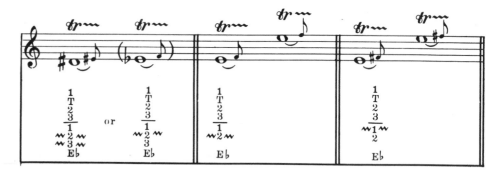

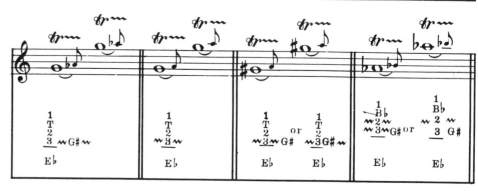

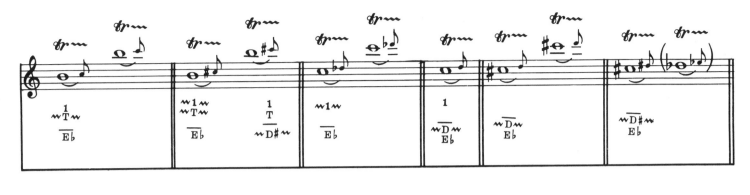

Musical Ornamentation (Embellishments)

The following treatment of ornamentation is by no means complete. It is presented here only as a guide to the execution of those ornaments which the student may encounter at this stage of his musical development. There are different manners of performing the same ornament.

The Trill (Shake)

The trill (or shake) consists of the rapid alternation of two tones. They are represented by the printed note (called the principal note) and the next tone above in the diatonic scale. The interval between the two tones may be either a half-step or a whole-step. The signs for the trill are *tr* and ⌀.

An accidental when used in conjunction with the trill sign affects the upper note of the trill.

Be sure to look up each trill fingering in the table.

✱ The asterisks indicate trill fingerings that differ from fundamental fingerings.

Grace Notes (Appoggiatura)

The grace notes are indicated by notes of a smaller size. They may be divided into two classes: long and short.

from "Sonata in A Major" Mozart

In instrumental music of recent composition the short grace notes should occupy as little time as possible and that value is taken preceding the principal note. They may be single, double, triple or quadruple, as the case may be. The single short grace note is printed as a small eighth note with a stroke through its hook. It is not to be accented. Use trill fingerings when fundamental fingerings are **too** difficult.

Excerpt from "Turkish March" Beethoven

The Mordent (℘)

The short mordent (℘) consists of a single rapid alternation of the principal note with its lower auxiliary. Two or more alternations are executed in the long mordent.

The short inverted mordent (℘) does not have the cross line. In it the lower auxiliary is replaced by the upper. It is the more commonly used mordent in music for the wind instruments.

The mordent takes its value from the principal note.

Short (single) Inverted Mordent   **Long (double) Inverted Mordent**

Excerpt from Schubert "Minuet"

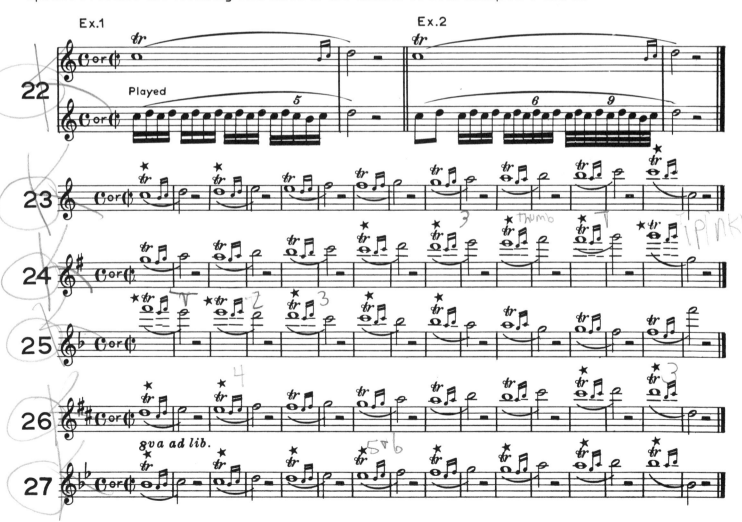

In trills of sufficient length a special ending is generally used whether indicated or not

The closing of the trill consists of two tones: the scale tone below the principal note and the principal note.

In long trills of a solo character it is good taste to commence slowly and gradually increase the speed. Practice the following exercises in the manner of both examples 1 and 2.

The Turn (Gruppetto)

The turn consists of four tones: the next scale tone above the principal tone, the principal tone it-self, the tone below the principal tone, and the principal tone again.

When the turn ∾ is placed to the right of the note, the principal tone is held almost to its full value, then the turn is played just before the next melody tone. In this case (Ex. 1,2,3,4 and 5) the four tones are of equal length.

When the turn is placed between a dotted note and another note having the same value as the dot (Ex.6 and 8), the turn is then played with the last note of the turn taking the place of the dot, making two notes of the same value. The turn sign after a dotted note will indicate that one melody note lies hidden in the dot.

Sometimes an accidental sign occurs with the turn, and in this case when written below the sign, it refers to the lowest tone of the turn, but when written above to the highest (Ex.1 and 2 below).

When the turn is placed over a note (Ex.3), the tones are usually played quickly, and the fourth tone is then held until the time value of the note has expired.

In the inverted turn (Ex.4) the order of tones is reversed, the lowest one coming first, the principal next, the highest third and the principal tone again, last. The inverted turn is indicated by the ordinary turn sign reversed ∾ or by ⌇.

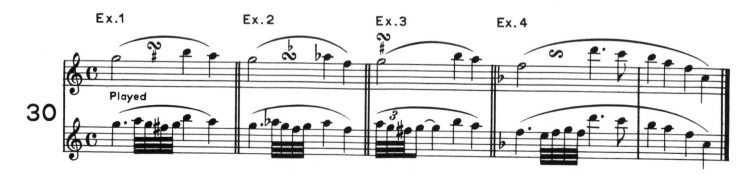

The Swan

cello

C. SAINT SAËNS

vibrato practice

Gavotte
from "Paris and Helen"

GLUCK

Saeterjentens Søndag

OLE BULL

Menuet

BOCCHERINI

Romance
Sans Paroles

SIVORI

Serenade

HAYDN

Andante cantabile

6